Written by Clive Gifford.
Illustrations by Nathan Daniels, Steve James,
Emiliano Migliardo, and Chris Dickason.
Cover typography based on designs by Thy Bui.

Amazing Facts: Kamala Harris
Copyright © 2024 by HarperCollins Publishers Limited
All rights reserved. Manufactured in Robbinsville, NJ, United States of America.
No part of this book may be used or reproduced in any manner whatsoever without written permission
except in the case of brief quotations embodied in critical articles and reviews.
For information address HarperCollins Children's Books,
a division of HarperCollins Publishers, 195 Broadway, New York, NY 10007.
www.harpercollinschildrens.com

ISBN 978-0-06-344094-4

24 25 26 27 28 PC/CWR 10 9 8 7 6 5 4 3 2 1

First published in Great Britain in 2024 by Red Shed, part of Farshore
An imprint of HarperCollinsPublishers 1 London Bridge Street, London SE1 9GF www.farshore.co.uk

HARPER
An Imprint of HarperCollinsPublishers

Did you know?

Kamala once used an ironing board as a campaign tool.

She has published cooking videos where she makes her favorite recipes.

Pearls are her favorite type of jewelry.

She was part of a dance group in high school.

Read on to discover over 100 fascinating and surprising facts about Kamala Harris, and her incredible life and work!

Kamala is named after a flower.

Kamala Devi Harris was born in Oakland, California, on October 20, 1964. Kamala and Devi are both ancient Indian names; Kamala means "lotus flower," and Devi means "goddess." Kamala's advice to pronounce her name is to say "comma-la." Try listening to her saying it to get it right!

Kamala grew up with an inspiring family.

Her father, Donald, is from the Caribbean island of Jamaica. He studied economics at the University of California, Berkeley—where he met Kamala's mother.

Her mom was a doctor and pioneering researcher.

Kamala's mother, Shyamala, grew up in India and went to Delhi University, but moved to California when she was 19 to continue studying. She had big dreams – her goal was to eradicate breast cancer.

Kamala's grandfather, P. V. Gopalan, worked as a civil servant in India and Zambia.

Civil servants work to keep government services, such as education and transport, running smoothly. Kamala visited her grandfather when she was a child – hearing him talk about justice and fairness influenced her to become a lawyer. Kamala has said he is one of her favorite people.

Young Kamala believed in freedom!

Kamala was born in the 1960s during the civil rights movement—a campaign for justice and equality for people of color. Her parents took part in lots of peaceful protests and often took Kamala with them in her stroller. When they asked her, "What do you want?" young Kamala would reply, "Fweedom!"

Kamala's mom loved cooking and experimenting with recipes.

One of Shyamala's family recipes was apples fried with bacon. Kamala re-created this recipe in a video in 2019, using it as a pancake topping!

Kamala has a little sister.

At the start of 1967, Kamala's sister, Maya Lakshmi Harris, was born. As a child, Maya loved eating leftover spaghetti carbonara for breakfast!

The Harris sisters grew up with many aunties and uncles.

This is what Kamala and Maya called the family's friends in California, even though they weren't related to them! Uncle Sherman taught Kamala how to play chess, which was useful for strategy and thinking ahead in politics.

Kamala and Maya spent most of their childhood with their mother.

Kamala's parents divorced when she was seven. She and Maya saw their dad at weekends and in the holidays.

Kamala grew up in sunny California... but she's lived in snowy Canada too.

When Kamala was 12 years old, Shyamala got a job in Montreal, Canada, as a cancer researcher. She, Kamala, and Maya all packed their bags, and off they went. Montreal is a cold, snowy city in the winter months, so they had to go shopping for cozy coats and mittens!

Kamala's mom was her biggest cheerleader.

When she was little, Kamala's mother, Shyamala, gave her confidence and encouraged her to support others. She said to her:

> Kamala, you may be the first to do many things, but make sure you're not the last.

Another of Shyamala's quotes went viral!

Kamala's mom once told her: "I don't know what's wrong with you young people. You think you just fell out of a coconut tree? You exist in the context of all in which you live and what came before you." In 2023, Kamala used the words in a speech. It was widely shared on social media through memes – Shyamala's wise words traveled all over the internet!

Kamala and Maya sometimes celebrated their "unbirthday."

If Maya or Kamala felt sad, their mom would throw them an "unbirthday" party with presents, cake, and dancing around the living room.

Kamala was inspired by her primary school teacher, Mrs. Frances Wilson.

Her first school was Thousand Oaks Elementary School in Berkeley, California. Mrs. Wilson taught the class about plants and animals and encouraged Kamala to learn about the world.

Kamala also went to a school where the main language was French.

Montreal, where the family lived, is in the French-speaking part of Canada. As Kamala hadn't grown up with French, she struggled with the new language, but she later moved to a school where English was spoken as well as French.

At elementary school, Kamala was full of energy.

She liked ball games, and her father encouraged her to run as fast as she could. Kamala often needed Band-Aids on her knees when she fell over!

Kamala took ballet classes at elementary school - and the dancing didn't stop when she left . . .

In high school, Kamala was a disco queen!

At Westmount High School, Montreal, Kamala formed an all-girl dance troupe called Midnight Magic. Kamala especially loved dancing to music by Diana Ross and Michael Jackson.

Kamala enjoyed playing soccer outside her apartment building in Montreal. When the landlord banned the games, 13-year-old Kamala led a protest – and it worked! The landlord agreed to allow soccer games.

Kamala loves the law.

Kamala wanted to become a lawyer so that she could get justice for those who were treated unfairly. Two of her heroes were Thurgood Marshall, the first African American to sit on the Supreme Court of the United States, and Constance Baker Motley, a pioneering Black lawyer.

Kamala worked in a mailroom.

One of Kamala's first part-time jobs was sorting letters in the mailroom of US Senator Alan Cranston, when she was 19-years-old.

Kamala once had a code name.

As a student, Kamala was a part-time tour guide at the Bureau of Engraving and Printing, which prints important documents. She was given a walkie-talkie and a code name: TG-10. It made her feel like a secret agent!

Lots of US presidents have had surprising jobs...

Barack Obama (2009–2017) sold ice cream.

Lyndon B. Johnson (1963–1969) shined shoes and herded goats.

Andrew Johnson (1865–1869) was a tailor.

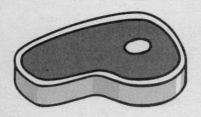

Gerald Ford (1974–1977) was a ranger at Yellowstone National Park. He drove the truck carrying meat to feed the park's wild bears!

Ronald Reagan (1981–1989) was a lifeguard and an actor.

Herbert Hoover (1929–1933) was a geologist and manager of an Australian gold mine.

Jimmy Carter (1977–1981) was a peanut farmer.

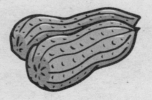

Kamala has two college degrees.

After graduating from high school, Kamala studied politics and economics at Howard University in Washington, DC, then law at Hastings College at the University of California. Kamala's elementary school teacher, Mrs. Wilson, was in the audience at her law school graduation ceremony. Kamala was very touched!

Kamala became a Democrat as a student.

We have two main political parties — the Democrats and the Republicans. Republican presidents include Abraham Lincoln, Ronald Reagan, and Donald Trump. Democratic presidents include Harry S. Truman, Bill Clinton, and Barack Obama.

Kamala failed an important law exam the first time around – but it didn't stop her!

The United States of America is made up of 50 states, each with their own local government and laws. To become a lawyer, you have to take an extra test in your state, called the bar exam, after graduating from college. Kamala didn't give up and passed her bar exam the next time. Go, Kamala!

Kamala isn't the only one to fail the bar exam the first time.

Other famous people who failed the first time include Michelle Obama (former First Lady), President John F. Kennedy, and President Franklin D. Roosevelt.

Kamala used to be a crime fighter!

Kamala's first job in law was in the office of the district attorney in Alameda County, California. The role involved taking lawbreakers to court. She often had to rush to a crime scene in the middle of the night to make sure evidence was collected in the right way.

Kamala first ran for office in San Francisco.

She has always dreamed big. In 2003, Kamala decided to take part in an election. She wanted to become the district attorney (DA) for the city of San Francisco, California. "Attorney" is another name for lawyer. The DA leads a big team of lawyers whose job is to prosecute criminals (put them on trial).

Kamala has lots of determination!

A poll showed only 6 percent of San Franciscans knew who she was. It wasn't easy to persuade them to vote for her over the other candidates!

Kamala used an ironing board in her campaign.

Kamala campaigned with three trusty tools: a campaign sign saying "Kamala Harris A Voice for Justice," a roll of duct tape, . . . and an ironing board. She'd drive to public places in San Francisco, pop up the ironing board, and tape the sign to the front of it. It made a perfect portable "desk" to stand behind!

Kamala loves pasta . . . and winning elections!

On the night of the district attorney election, Kamala went out for an Italian meal with her trusted group of campaign volunteers. They ate pasta and used the paper tablecloth to keep a tally of the votes as the results came in.

Kamala made it to the runoff (a vote between the top two candidates), then gained 56.5 percent of the vote. She'd won her first political election!

Kamala supports LGBTQ+ rights.

As district attorney for San Francisco, Kamala made national news by officiating (performing) some of the first same-sex weddings in the country.

Kamala had a big ambition.

In 2010, Kamala ran to be the attorney general for California – the top lawyer in the state.

She was a surprise winner.

She was up against Republican Steve Cooley – who assumed that he had won! On election night, Cooley made a victory speech, and several newspapers printed that he'd gotten the job. But after all the votes were counted, it turned out that Kamala had won by 74,000 votes.

Kamala made history.

On January 3, 2011, she became the first woman and the first person of color to be elected as California's attorney general.

Kamala helped homeowners.

As California's attorney general, Kamala battled hard for people who had been let down by banks and lost their homes. The banks offered $4 billion in compensation . . . but Kamala wanted more for the homeowners. In 2012, after fierce negotiations, Kamala got the banks to pay $20.4 billion. That's five times as much!

Kamala met her husband, Doug, while she was attorney general.

In 2013, one of Kamala's friends set her up on a blind date with another lawyer, Doug Emhoff. Doug left Kamala a long voicemail before they met – he thought she'd be put off, but she wasn't!

Doug proposed while Kamala was ordering takeout.

Less than a year after she met Doug, Kamala was having a busy day packing for a flight to Florence, Italy – the pair were going on a romantic vacation. She was deciding between takeout options when Doug got down on one knee. He had planned to propose when they arrived in Italy, but he couldn't wait!

Kamala was married by her sister.

Kamala and Doug got married on August 22, 2014, in Santa Barbara, California. Her sister, Maya, officiated the ceremony and her niece, Meena, read a poem by the inspiring American writer Maya Angelou.

Kamala became... Momala!

Kamala was delighted to become a stepmom to Doug's two children, Cole and Ella Emhoff, who were 19 and 15 at the time. She didn't want to be called their stepmother, so she and the two children came up with a different name: Momala.

Kamala speaks up for blended families.

In a speech in August 2020, she said, "I've had a lot of titles over my career . . . but 'Momala' will always be one of those that means the most."

Ella Emhoff was named after jazz singer Ella Fitzgerald . . .

Ella is now a model and fashion designer who loves to knit.

. . . and Cole Emhoff's name was inspired by jazz musician John Coltrane.

Kamala's parents also liked listening to this jazz musician. Cole has gone on to work in TV and film production.

Kamala is comfy in Converse . . .

Kamala often chooses sneakers over high heels. She has lots of different pairs of Converse classic Chuck Taylors – they come in useful when she's on her feet all day campaigning!

. . . and she sometimes personalizes them with badges.

At one rally in 2020 for the presidential election, Kamala pinned badges to her sneakers saying "Stop Hate" and "Love 2020."

Pearls are Kamala's favorite type of jewelry.

One of her mother's college tutors gave Kamala a string of pearls as a gift when she was younger. She's loved them ever since and can often be seen wearing pearls during speeches or at events.

In 2016, Kamala was elected to Congress!

Each of the 50 states is represented in Congress (a part of the government) by two senators, who are elected by the public. They vote on things like passing laws or appointing judges to courts. California chose Kamala as one of its representatives.

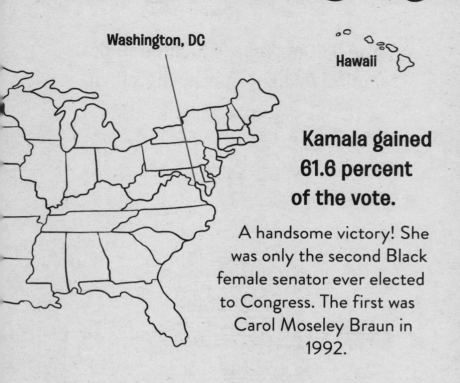

Kamala gained 61.6 percent of the vote.

A handsome victory! She was only the second Black female senator ever elected to Congress. The first was Carol Moseley Braun in 1992.

Congress is made up of two parts.

As well as the Senate, where Kamala was elected, there's the House of Representatives. Together, they make up Congress. Both parts work together to pass laws and keep the country running smoothly.

The US Congress is located in the Capitol Building in Washington, DC.

The building has about 540 rooms.
It can be easy to get lost!

The Capitol Building's dome is HUGE.

It took nearly nine million pounds of cast iron to construct the dome. That's about the same weight as 20 Statues of Liberty!

In the Senate Chamber, Democrats sit on the left and Republicans sit on the right, all at wooden desks.

The Senate Chamber is where senators sit to make decisions – one party on either side of a central aisle. When Senator Wayne Morse left the Republican party in 1952, he brought a folding chair and sat in the middle of the aisle to show he was independent.

One desk in the Senate Chamber holds a secret: it is crammed full of sweets!

Desk 80 is known as the "candy desk." A Republican senator named George Murphy started the tradition in 1965, and the Democrats joined in with their own candy desk in the 1980s.

The Capitol Building has its own subway...

Senators and their staff get to ride on their own underground train system, built in 1909. The Senate subway shuttles them speedily between their office buildings and the Capitol Building.

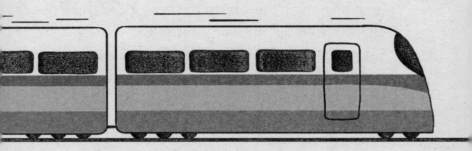

...and bathtubs!

In the 1850s, many senators lived in Washington, DC, boardinghouses without running water. To stop them from stinking up Congress, marble baths were installed in the basement from 1858.

Congress has one of the biggest libraries in the world.

The Library of Congress holds more than 173 million books. Around 10,000 new items are added to its collection every day!

The Library of Congress holds the world's biggest comic book collection.

There are more than 165,000 comics! The library is also home to President Thomas Jefferson's recipe for vanilla ice cream. Yum!

When Kamala became a senator, she needed somewhere to live in Washington, DC.

She rented an apartment and started out with very little furniture — just a bed, two stools, a sofa bed for visitors, . . . and a giant TV!

Kamala has been part of many important committees.

Congress has many committees that make sure proper attention is paid to different issues. Kamala has contributed to many of them, including the Budget committee and the Environment and Public Works committee (which looks at developments such as roads and public buildings).

Kamala has worked hard to protect the environment.

As attorney general, she prosecuted companies for harming the environment. As a senator and as vice president, she supported renewable energy and reducing greenhouse gas emissions. She has called the climate crisis "one of the most urgent matters of our time."

The US chooses a president once every four years.

The president is the US's head of state. Presidents can hold the top job for up to two terms (eight years). Each president appoints a vice president, who acts as their deputy.

In 2019, Kamala started her first campaign to be a presidential candidate.

Kamala put herself forward as a presidential candidate for the Democratic party, along with several other politicians. Her sister, Maya, headed Kamala's campaign, and her passionate supporters are known online as the KHive – like the Beyhive (fans of Beyoncé).

Kamala's campaign took a new direction.

She didn't receive quite enough support to carry on with her own campaign, but in August 2020, Joe Biden picked her to be his running mate. Presidential candidates pick a running mate to help them campaign and become their vice president if they get elected.

Kamala and Joe were the winning ticket.

The 2020 presidential election was close. In the end, after lots of counting and recounting, the results were in. Joe Biden had received 81,283,501 votes and his opponent, Donald Trump, had 74,223,975. Joe and Kamala had won!

Kamala's win was a historic moment!

On January 20, 2021, Kamala was sworn in as vice president. She became the first ever female vice president of the United States. She was also the first Black American and the first South Asian American to be elected into this position.

US presidential elections are some of the biggest in the world...

In the 2020 election, where the main candidates were Donald Trump and Joe Biden, 158,429,631 people voted. That's more than double the population of France!

... but they weren't always so huge.

In early presidential elections, far fewer people had their say – partly because the population was smaller and also because not everyone was allowed to vote. In 1824, just 350,671 people voted for their favorite candidate.

Many people in the US had to fight hard for their right to vote.

Women weren't allowed to vote in all US states until 1920. People of color faced discrimination in elections until a law protecting their right to vote was passed in 1965. Today, every US citizen aged 18 years or over, who has not been found guilty of certain crimes, has the right to vote.

The official home of the US president is the White House.

This famous building is on Pennsylvania Avenue in northwestern Washington, DC. It is not just a home – hundreds of advisors and staff work here!

Presidents have made a lot of changes to the White House over time.

Today, the White House has 132 rooms, 35 bathrooms, 8 staircases, and 412 doors. It also has a bowling alley, a gym, a movie theater, and a flower shop, where the White House chief floral designer creates beautiful floral arrangements to decorate the building.

The White House needs a lot of paint to stay white!

It takes approximately 570 gallons of Whisper White paint from Germany to coat the White House in its gleaming white colour.

The White House is near the Potomac River.

John Quincy Adams, who served as the USA's sixth president from 1825–1829, liked to take an early morning dip in the river . . . in the nude!

Kamala loves dancing ... but not everyone in the White House did.

Dancing was banned in the White House during the term of James K. Polk, America's eleventh president (1845–1849). His wife, Sarah, disapproved of it.

The White House sits on grounds about the size of ten football fields.

When Woodrow Wilson was president from 1913–1921, the grass on the large North Lawn was kept short by a flock of 48 sheep!

Other animal inhabitants have included two black bear cubs, a hyena, a pygmy hippo, and an alligator.

These animals were gifts from world leaders to US presidents. The alligator was allegedly kept in a bathtub during John Quincy Adams's presidency in the 1820s! As the animals were tricky to look after, they were eventually given homes in zoos.

The vice president lives in a different "white house."

It's not the White House – but it *is* painted white! The vice president's mansion is on the grounds of the US Naval Observatory in Washington, DC. Kamala and Doug moved there in 2021.

When Kamala became vice president, her husband got a new title as well.

Doug Emhoff became the first ever Second Gentleman.

The first vice president to live in the US Naval Observatory house was Walter Mondale.

He served with President Jimmy Carter from 1977–1981. Before then, vice presidents and their families lived in their own homes.

Since 1961, vice presidents have all used the same desk.

The mahogany desk was first used by Theodore Roosevelt in 1902. It now sits in the Eisenhower Executive Office Building, to the west of the White House. At the end of their term, each vice president signs the inside of the center drawer. Kamala's signature adds to the list!

Kamala has hosted politicians...

Kamala has entertained important world leaders at the vice president's house, such as former German leader Angela Merkel, who ate breakfast with her in 2021.

...hip-hop stars...

In 2023, Kamala hosted a big party to celebrate the 50th anniversary of hip-hop. More than 400 guests enjoyed performances from legendary hip-hop artists, including MC Lyte, Doug E. Fresh, Lil Wayne, and Roxanne Shanté.

. . . and astronauts.

Kamala hosted a space-themed event in 2022 for local schoolkids. Some real-life astronauts came along to join the fun!

Kamala loves books AND she's an author!

Kamala published a children's book in 2019 called *Superheroes Are Everywhere*. Based on her own experiences, it shows young readers that everyone has the power to make a difference.

One of Kamala's favorite books is *The Lion, the Witch and the Wardrobe.*

In 2019, she revealed the books she has found most inspiring and enjoyable in her life, including this classic by C. S. Lewis. Another of her much-loved books is *Song of Solomon* by award-winning African American author Toni Morrison.

As vice president, Kamala once ran the USA . . . for 85 minutes.

One of the vice president's jobs is to take over if the president dies or is too ill to work. In 2021, Kamala stepped up while President Joe Biden had a routine operation.

Kamala is an expert tiebreaker.

Another of the vice president's jobs is serving as president of the Senate. Many votes take place here, for example, to decide if laws should be created or changed. If a vote is tied, the vice president has the deciding vote. This happens more often than you might think – by the end of July 2024, Kamala had made the final decision on 33 votes!

Kamala isn't the only one making history.

In 2022, Ketanji Brown Jackson was elected as a judge in the Supreme Court (the highest court in the USA). Jackson was the first Black woman to be offered this role – a historic moment. Kamala was present when the Senate voted to confirm Ketanji into the new role – during the vote, Kamala wrote a letter to her goddaughter about how much pride and joy she felt in the moment.

The vice president has their own plane.

This aircraft, named Air Force Two, is a modified Boeing 757 with desks, a well-stocked kitchen, and even a bed. Long flights are good times to work or get some much-needed rest!

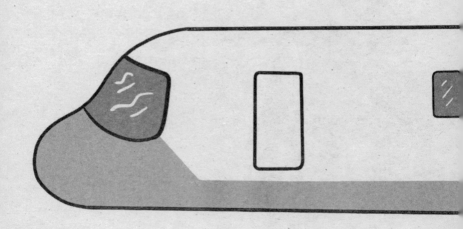

In her first three years of being vice president, Kamala flew nearly 400,000 miles on official business.

That's the same as flying around the world 15 times!

Kamala loves visiting new places.

One thing she likes to do in new countries is visit their Supreme Court – or other important court buildings.

She gets to eat some incredible food.

In 2021, Kamala visited Singapore and had an amazing lunch! Singaporeans had sent in menu suggestions on social media. The meal included rojak (salad served with a sweet and sour sauce), laksa (spicy noodle soup), sambar (lentil stew), and teh tarik (hot milky tea). She loved it!

Kamala has a plant named after her.

While visiting Singapore, she was presented with a new type of orchid by the country's prime minister at the time, Lee Hsien Loong. It was named in her honor: *Papilionanda Kamala Harris*.

Kamala is a champion handshaker...

Presidents and vice presidents have a lot of hand shaking to do. They're often at events, meeting and greeting people.

... but she'll have to work hard to break President Theodore Roosevelt's record!

At a New Year's Day event in 1906, President Theodore Roosevelt shook hands with a record-breaking 8,513 visitors.

Kamala loves rom-coms...

Kamala doesn't get much time off, but when she does, she loves watching a good romantic comedy with her husband, Doug.

. . . and superhero movies!

For her 56th birthday, Kamala joined a fundraising Zoom call with actors from the Avengers superhero film series. She was thrilled!

Kamala loves to cook...

In 2019 and 2020, Kamala posted a series of videos on YouTube called "Cooking with Kamala," where she cooked dishes such as masala dosa (a type of pancake from southern India) and tuna melts. She also loves making roast chicken for Sunday dinner!

...but she's had kitchen catastrophes too!

As children, Kamala and her sister spent a lot of time with one of their mother's friends, Regina Shelton. One day, Kamala baked lemon bars to share with her . . . only she used salt instead of sugar! Mrs. Shelton took a bite, and to avoid hurting the young girl's feelings said, "That's delicious . . . maybe a little too much salt . . . but really delicious." Kamala is a far better cook now!

In 2024, Kamala became the first Black woman and the first South Asian person to run as a US presidential candidate.

On July 21, 2024, President Joe Biden announced that he wouldn't be running for a second term in charge. He backed Kamala to replace him as the Democrats' candidate for the 2024 election.

Kamala's campaign was super speedy!

Most presidential campaigns go on for almost two years – but Kamala's lasted just three months!

Vice presidents often go on to become presidents.

Many vice presidents of the US have gone on to become president – some very quickly! In 1841, John Tyler got the top job after just a month as vice president. This was after President William Henry Harrison died from pneumonia.

For her campaign launch, Kamala used music by another Black female icon - Beyoncé!

The big launch happened at her campaign headquarters in Wilmington, Delaware. Kamala's first campaign TV ad used Beyoncé's song "Freedom."

Kamala's campaign received donations of more than $81 million in just 24 hours.

That's the most ever raised by a presidential campaign in a single day. By the end of the first week, she had raised around $200 million.

As a presidential candidate, Kamala got to pick her own running mate.

A running mate is the person who becomes a candidate's vice president if they are elected. Kamala unveiled her choice on August 6, 2024 – it was Tim Walz, the governor of Minnesota since 2018.

Tim was a teacher for almost 20 years.

He worked as a geography teacher at Mankato West High School in Minnesota – Tim credits his students for encouraging him to get involved in politics! He also coached the school's football team.

He served in the US National Guard for 24 years.

This reserve military force helps in national disasters and other emergencies.

Tim stands up for the LGBTQ+ community.

Tim helped start a Gay-Straight Alliance at his school – a space where LGBTQ+ students could feel accepted and supported.

Kamala and Tim were endorsed by Barack and Michelle Obama.

Kamala was already friends with Barack, the 44th president of the US – but it made her day when she got a call from him and his wife, Michelle, endorsing her to run as president. The pair later endorsed her running mate, Tim Walz, as well.

Kamala is brat.

Lots of music stars endorsed Kamala for president, including Charli XCX. Her lime-green June 2024 album *Brat* was hugely popular, and she backed Kamala on social media, saying "Kamala IS brat." The campaign turned their website pages lime green to match the album.

Abraham Lincoln

George Washington

Kamala is a role model for women.

Most US politicians in the past have been men (including all the presidents). Kamala uses her position to inspire women – in a 2019 interview, she gave some advice to young women and girls:

"You are powerful and your voice matters."

John F. Kennedy

Theodore Roosevelt

Kamala has been inspired by female politicians from US history.

One of her major inspirations is Shirley Chisholm. In 1968, this former nursery school teacher became the first African American woman to be elected to the US Congress.

Shirley fought for underrepresented voices to be heard, saying: "If they don't give you a seat at the table, bring in a folding chair."

The very first US president was George Washington.

Until 1776, the US was ruled by Great Britain. George Washington led the army that defeated the British, making the US independent! He served as president from 1789 to 1797 and worked hard to help set up the government and laws that would run the new independent country.

George Washington is the only president to have a US state named after him.

Washington, a state in the northwest, was given this name in the 1800s.

He loved dancing!

George took politics seriously . . . but he also enjoyed a good party. He often stayed up late to dance the night away.

Washington fought in several battles.

He had some near misses. During the Battle of the Monongahela in 1755, four bullets flew past him, close enough to pierce his coat!

The two youngest presidents were Theodore Roosevelt and John F. Kennedy.

Theodore Roosevelt was the youngest ever president at 42 years old. He was vice president when President William McKinley was assassinated and took over automatically. John F. Kennedy was the youngest president to run as a candidate and be elected. On the day he was inaugurated (officially made president), he was 43 years old. Kamala Harris was 59 when she launched her presidential campaign.

Joe Biden was the oldest US president.

When Joe was born in 1942, World War II was still being fought. He became the president when he was 78 years old.

Presidents today must be at least 35 years old.

They must also be a citizen who was born in the United States and have lived in the country for at least 14 years.

Some great US presidents were lawyers, just like Kamala.

Abraham Lincoln, president from 1861 to 1865, had been a lawyer. Lincoln was also postmaster for the town of New Salem, Illinois. He sometimes delivered important letters himself by carrying them in his tall hat.

Some US presidents were military leaders.

President Dwight D Eisenhower led military troops in World War II.

Some had careers in business.

Donald Trump, who became president in 2017, ran his own company. He also ran as the Republican candidate against Kamala in 2024.

Many held jobs in government.

Fifteen presidents held the job of vice president before eventually getting the top job.

Kamala believes you can do anything!

One of Kamala's top tips is to "eat no for breakfast." She means, when people say things like "you can't do it," "you're too young," or "no one has done it like that before," ... don't give up. Double up your efforts and go for your dream!